Handy Oklahoma Genealogy Handbook

I0450513

Gary L. Morris

©2015 Gary L. Morris

ISBN-13: 978-1507786536

ISBN-10: 1507786530

Table of Contents

Notes

Genealogical Research in Oklahoma

As it is one of the longest populated American states, there are many genealogical records and resources available for tracing your family history in Oklahoma. Because there are so many records held at many different locations, tracking down the records for your ancestor can be an ominous task. Don't worry though, we know just where they are, and we'll show you which records you'll need, while helping you to understand:

1. What they are
2. Where to find them
3. How to use them

These records can be found both online and off, so we'll introduce you to online websites, indexes and databases, as well as brick-and-mortar repositories and other institutions that will help with your research in Oklahoma. So that you will have a more comprehensive understanding of these records, we have provided a brief history of the "Sooner State" to illustrate what type of records may have been generated during specific time periods. That information will assist you in pinpointing times and locations on which to focus the search for your Oklahoma ancestors and their records.

A Brief History of Oklahoma

When the first Europeans, Spanish conquistadores, led by Francisco Vasquez de Coronado and Hernando de Soto, arrived in the sixteenth century, there were but a few scattered Native American tribes inhabiting the area. The area remained largely unsettled until the early nineteenth century when it became part of the Louisiana Purchase in 1803. Even then settlement was sparse and the area became known as Indian Country when tribes from the southeastern United States were resettled there under the Indian Removal Act in 1830.

Four thousand Native Americans died on the journey to Oklahoma, gaining it name the "Trail of Tears." Those that survived the journey however, Native Americans from the Five Civilized Tribes – Chickasaw, Cherokee, Creek, Choctaw, and Seminole, prospered in the region between the time of removal up until the Civil War period.

The Five Civilized Tribes settled the eastern part of Oklahoma comprising nearly half of the state. The area offered luxurious vegetation and rich, fertile soil, which attracted many white farmers to the area as well. The methods the white settlers used depleted the spoil however, leading the way to the area becoming known as the "Dust Bowl" in the 1930's. People and goods passed through the area in increasing numbers during the mid to late nineteenth century, and forts were established at Ft. Gibson, Ft. Towson, and Fort Supply between 1824 and the 1880's.

By the time the Civil War arrived, some of the members of the Five Civilized Tribes were slaveholders, and they allied themselves with the Confederacy. The Union Army captured Fort Gibson in 1863, after which time the Union controlled half of the Indian Territory. Between the end of the Civil war and the 1880's, the eastern tribes were steadily removed by the federal government from their lands, which were especially attractive to white settlers and railroad developers. This period saw increasing skirmishes between federal troops and Indians, ending in the famous massacre of the Cheyenne by Col. George Custer and his troops at the Battle of Washita in 1868.

White settlers continued their clamor for Indian lands, and in 1889 the federal government opened land western Oklahoma formerly reserved for the Cheyenne, Cherokee, and Fox to white settlement. The biggest onslaught of white settlers to the area occurred in 1893 when close to 100,000 settlers flooded the region. The western part of Oklahoma was designated the Oklahoma Territory in 1890, while most of the eastern region remained in possession of the Five Civilized Tribes.

A bill for statehood was introduced in 1892 but was resisted by the Native American tribes. The Indians attempted to form their own independent state during the interim, but when that movement was defeated in 1905, Oklahoma received statehood two years later on November 16, 1907.

Important Dates in Oklahoma History

1803 – Part of Louisiana Purchase

1812 – Part of Missouri Territory

1819 – Part of Arkansas Territory

1830 – Organized as Indian Territory

1831 – Five Civilized Tribes forcibly removed to the area

1861 – Most of Five Civilized Tribes side with the Confederacy

1889 – Part of Oklahoma opened for white settlement

1890 – Organized as Oklahoma Territory

1893 – Land belonging to the Cherokees opened for settlement

1906 – Most tribal governments and reservations are liquidated

1907 - Statehood

Famous Battles Fought in Oklahoma

There have been very few battles fought within the borders of modern day Oklahoma, though the Civil War battles of **Fort Wayne**, **Cabin Creek**, and **Honey Springs** were all important Union victories. The famous massacre of Cheyenne Indians, the **Battle of Washita River**, took place near modern day Cheyenne, Oklahoma. .

These battle accounts that exist can be very effective in uncovering the military records of your ancestor. They can tell you what regiments fought in which battles, and often include the names and ranks of many officers and enlisted men.

Fort Wayne:
http://digital.library.okstate.edu/encyclopedia/entries/F/FO048.html

Cabin Creek: http://www.okhistory.org/sites/cabincreek

Honey Springs: http://www.civilwar.org/battlefields/honey-springs.html

Battle of Washita River:
http://digital.library.okstate.edu/encyclopedia/entries/W/WA037.html

Common Oklahoma Genealogical Issues and Resources to Overcome Them

Boundary Changes: Boundary changes are a common obstacle when researching Oklahoma ancestors. You could be searching for an ancestor's record in one county when in fact it is stored in a different one due to historical county boundary changes.

The **Atlas of Historical County Boundaries** can help you to overcome that problem. It provides a chronological listing of every boundary change that has occurred in the history of Oklahoma.

Atlas of Historical County Boundaries: http://publications.newberry.org/ahcbp/documents/OK_Consolidated _Chronology.htm#Consolidated_Chronology

Name Changes: Surname changes, variations, and misspellings can complicate genealogical research. It is important to check all spelling variations. Soundex, a program that indexes names by sound, is a useful first step, but you can't rely on it completely as some name variations result in different Soundex codes. The surnames could be different, but the first name may be different too. You can also find records filed under initials, middle names, and nicknames as well, so you will need to **get creative with surname variations** and spellings in order to cover all the possibilities. For help with surname variations read our instructional article on **How to Use Soundex**.

get creative with surname variations: http://obituarieshelp.org/blog/?p=634

How to Use Soundex: http://obituarieshelp.org/blog/?p=505

Oklahoma Genealogical Organizations and Archives

Genealogical resources include not only records, but the organizations that house them, or can direct you to them. These institutions include: *Archives, Libraries, Genealogical Societies, Family History Centers, Universities, Churches, and Museums.*

Following are links to their websites, their physical addresses, and a summary of the records you can find there.

Archives and Libraries

Oklahoma Department of Libraries (State Archives) – military records, homestead records, county histories, periodicals, indexes, and reference works

200 N.E. 18th Street
Oklahoma City, OK 73105-3298
Telephone: 405-522-3579
Fax: 405-525-7804

Oklahoma Department of Libraries:
http://www.odl.state.ok.us/oar/resources/genealogy.htm

Lawton Public Library - Federal census schedules, local and area newspapers from 1901, Indian-Pioneer History Collection, Indian records, probate records, family histories, vital records, Oklahoma Tract Books with surname index, and research reference aids

110 S.W. 4th Street
Lawton, OK 73105-3298
Telephone: 405-581-3450

Lawton Public Library:
http://www.cityof.lawton.ok.us/library/genealogy.htm

University of Oklahoma - Indian-Pioneer Papers, historical manuscripts, county records, Spanish, Indian, military, Civil War, newspapers, cattle trails, ranching, mining, and oil production records

OU Great Reading Room
630 Parrington Oval, Room 452
Norman, OK 73019
Telephone: 405-325-3641
Fax: 405-325-2943

University of Oklahoma: http://libraries.ou.edu/locations/?id=22

Oklahoma Genealogical and Historical Societies

Genealogical and historical societies have access to extensive catalogues of genealogical data. They are also able to offer expert guidance for genealogical researchers. Many members are professional genealogists who are most willing to share their expertise in finding ancestors.

Oklahoma Historical Society – Native American records, census records, vital records, military records, probate records, historical newspapers, city directories, historical maps and photographs

800 Nazih Zudhi Drive
Oklahoma City, OK 73105
Telephone: 405-522-5225
Fax: 405-521-2492

Oklahoma Historical Society:
http://www.okhistory.org/research/genealogy?full

Tulsa Genealogical Society Library - Bibles, cemeteries, obituaries, family histories, city directories, vital records indexes

9136 East 31st Street
Tulsa, OK 74145
Telephone: 918-627-4224

Tulsa Genealogical Society Library:
http://www.tulsagenealogy.org/library/

Oklahoma Mailing Lists

Mailing lists are internet based facilities that use email to distribute a single message to all who subscribe to it. When information on a particular surname, new records, or any other important genealogy information related to the mailing list topic becomes available, the subscribers are alerted to it. Joining a mailing list is an excellent way to stay up to date on Oklahoma genealogy research topics. Rootsweb have an extensive listing of **Oklahoma Mailing Lists** on a variety of topics.

Oklahoma Mailing Lists:
http://lists.rootsweb.ancestry.com/index/usa/OK/misc.html

Oklahoma Message Boards

A message board is another internet based facility where people can post questions about a specific genealogy topic and have it answered by other genealogists. If you have questions about a surname, record type, or research topic, you can post your question and other researchers and genealogists will help you with the answer. Be sure to check back regularly, as the answers are not emailed to you. The Oklahoma message boards at **Rootsweb** are completely free to use.

Rootsweb:
http://boards.rootsweb.com/localities.northam.usa.states/mb.ashx

Oklahoma Newspapers and Periodicals

Many genealogy periodicals and historical newspapers contain reprinted copies of family genealogies, transcripts of family Bible records, information about local records and archives, census indexes, church records, queries, land records, obituaries, court records, cemetery records, and wills. The following sites have historical Oklahoma newspapers and periodicals that you can search online or on-site.

Oklahoma Historical Society – collection of historical newspapers from 1819-present

800 Nazih Zudhi Drive
Oklahoma City, OK 73105
Telephone: 405-522-5225
Fax: 405-521-2492

Oklahoma Historical Society:
http://www.okhistory.org/research/genealogy?full

Lawton Public Library - local and area newspapers from 1901

110 S.W. 4th Street
Lawton, OK 73105-3298
Telephone: 405-581-3450

Lawton Public Library:
http://www.cityof.lawton.ok.us/library/genealogy.htm

GenealogyBank.com – free searchable database of Oklahoma newspaper archives, 1871-1923

GenealogyBank.com:
http://www.genealogybank.com/gbnk/newspapers/explore/USA/Oklahoma/

The Online Books Page – links to historical Oklahoma books and periodicals available for viewing online

The Online Books Page: http://onlinebooks.library.upenn.edu

Library of Congress Digital Newspaper Directory – free searchable database of historical U.S. newspapers dating from 1690-present

Library of Congress Digital Newspaper Directory: http://chroniclingamerica.loc.gov/search/titles/

NewspaperArchive.com – largest online database of historical newspapers in the world.

NewspaperArchive.com: http://newspaperarchive.com/

Historical Oklahoma Maps and Gazetteers

Maps are an integral part of genealogical research. They help us to locate landmarks, towns, cities, parishes, states, provinces, waterways and roads and streets. They also help us to determine when and where boundary changes might have taken place, and give us a visualization of the area we're researching in.

For locating place names, a gazetteer is the best possible resource for any genealogist. Gazetteers are also sometimes called "place name dictionaries", and can help you to locate the area in which you need to conduct research. Below are links to the maps and gazetteers for research in Oklahoma.

Peabody GNIS Service – Oklahoma:
http://peabody.research.yale.edu/cgi-bin/Query.GNIS?ST=Oklahoma&SU=1

Color Landform Atlas – Oklahoma:
http://fermi.jhuapl.edu/states/ok_0.html

1985 U.S. Atlas: http://www.livgenmi.com/1895/OK/

Oklahoma Hometown Locator:
http://oklahoma.hometownlocator.com/

Oklahoma City Directories

.

City directories are similar to telephone directories in that they list the residents of a particular area. The difference though is what is important to genealogists, and that is they pre-date telephone directories. You can find an ancestor's information such as their street address, place of employment, occupation, or the name of their spouse. A one-stop-shop for finding city directories in Oklahoma is the **Oklahoma Online Historical Directories** which contains a listing of every available online historical directory related to Oklahoma.

Oklahoma Online Historical Directories:
https://sites.google.com/site/onlinedirectorysite/Home/usa/ok

Oklahoma Historical Society – collection of Oklahoma city directories dating from late nineteenth century to present

800 Nazih Zudhi Drive
Oklahoma City, OK 73105
Telephone: 405-522-5225
Fax: 405-521-2492

Oklahoma Historical Society:
http://www.okhistory.org/research/directories

Oklahoma Genealogical Records

Birth, Death, Marriage and Divorce Records – Also known as vital records, birth, death, and marriage certificates are the most basic, yet most important records attached to your ancestor. The reason for their importance is that they not only place your ancestor in a specific place at a definite time, but potentially connect the individual to other relatives. Below is a list of repositories and websites where you can find Oklahoma vital records.

Some counties in Oklahoma kept birth and death records as early as 1891, but the majority did not comply until after statehood in 1907. Those earliest records, along with marriage and divorce records from 1890 to present, can be found at **Oklahoma District Courts**.

Oklahoma District Courts:
http://www.oscn.net/applications/oscn/start.asp?viewType=COURT
S

The statewide registration of births and deaths began in Oklahoma in 1908. Those records may be requested from:

Oklahoma State Department of Health
Vital Records Service
1000 Northeast 10th Street, Room 111
Oklahoma City, OK 73117
Telephone: 405-271-4040

Oklahoma State Department of Health:
http://www.ok.gov/health/Birth_and_Death_Certificates/Genealogist
s/index.html

Oklahoma Historical Society – Death, marriage and divorce records dating from 1889

800 Nazih Zudhi Drive
Oklahoma City, OK 73105
Telephone: 405-522-5225
Fax: 405-521-2492

Oklahoma Historical Society:
http://www.okhistory.org/research/genealogy?full

Lawton Public Library – County Marriage records, 1901-1981; county birth records, 1918-1935; county death records, 1918-1945; Marriage licenses, 1893-1974

110 S.W. 4th Street
Lawton, OK 73105-3298
Telephone: 405-581-3450

Lawton Public Library:
http://www.cityof.lawton.ok.us/library/genealogy.htm

Family Search has the following indexes which can be searched online for free:**riages, 1890-1995**

Oklahoma Marriages, 1870-1930:
https://familysearch.org/search/collection/1681007

Oklahoma, County Marriages, 1890-1995:
https://familysearch.org/search/collection/1709399

Census Reports

Census records are among the most important genealogical documents for placing your ancestor in a particular place at a specific time. Like BDM records, they can also lead you to other ancestors, particularly those who were living under the authority of the head of household.

Federal census records for Oklahoma exist from 1910 –1930 and can be found at:

Lawton Public Library - 1890 Oklahoma Territorial Census, 1890 Special Census schedule of Union Army Veterans and their widows, 1900 Oklahoma Territory Census, 1900 Indian Territory Census, 1910-1930 Federal State Census

110 S.W. 4th Street
Lawton, OK 73105-3298
Telephone: 405-581-3450

Lawton Public Library:
http://www.cityof.lawton.ok.us/library/genealogy.htm

Oklahoma Historical Society – 1890 Oklahoma Territorial census

800 Nazih Zudhi Drive
Oklahoma City, OK 73105
Telephone: 405-522-5225
Fax: 405-521-2492

Oklahoma Historical Society:
http://www.okhistory.org/research/1890

National Archives – Federal census Schedules for all states, 1790-1940

8601 Adelphi Road
College Park, MD 20740-6001
Tel: 1-866-272-6272

National Archives: http://www.archives.gov/research/census/

The **Free Census Project** has transcribed many Oklahoma indexes and new material is added daily

Free Census Project: http://usgwcensus.org/cenfiles/ok.htm

Access Genealogy – Oklahoma county census records dating from 1860-1930

Access Genealogy:
http://www.accessgenealogy.com/census/oklahoma-census-records.htm

African American Census Schedules Online – slave schedules, mortality schedules, slave-owners census

African American Census Schedules Online:
http://www.afrigeneas.com/aacensus/

Native Americans in Census Records (US National Archives):
http://www.archives.gov/research/census/native-americans/

Oklahoma Church Records

Church and synagogue records are a valuable resource, especially for baptisms, marriages, and burials that took place before 1900. You will need to at least have an idea of your ancestor's religious denomination, and in most cases you will have to visit a brick and mortar establishment to view them.

Most church records are kept by the individual church, although in some denominations, records are placed in a regional archive or maintained at the diocesan level. Local Historical Societies are sometimes the repository for the state's older church records. Below are links archives that maintain church records, as well as a few databases that can be viewed online.

The **Family History Library** contains many church records from a variety of denominations on microfilm.

Family History Library:
http://familysearch.org/learn/wiki/en/Family_History_Library

Central Repositories for Denominational Records

Church of Jesus Christ of Latter-day Saints (Mormons)

Early Mormon Church records for Oklahoma can be found on film located at the LDS Family History Library in Salt Lake City and can be searched via the **Family History Library Catalog**

Family History Library Catalog:
https://familysearch.org/eng/Library/FHLC/frameset_fhlc.asp

Baptist

Southern Baptist Convention
901 Commerce Street #400
Nashville, TN 37203-3699
Phone: (615) 244-0344
Fax: (615) 782-4821

Southern Baptist Convention: http://www.sbhla.org/

Disciples of Christ

Disciples of Christ Historical Society
1101 Nineteenth Avenue, South
Nashville, TN 37212
Phone: (615) 327-1444
Fax: (615) 327-1445

Disciples of Christ Historical Society:
http://www.discipleshistory.org/

Methodist

United Methodist Church Archives
P.O. Box 127 Drew University
36 Madison Ave.
Madison, NJ 07940-3189
Telephone: 973-408-3189
Fax: 973-408-3909
E-mail: research@gcah.org

United Methodist Church Archives:
http://www.gcah.org/site/c.ghKJI0PHIoE/b.2858857/k.BF4D/Home.
htm

Moravian Church

The Moravian Archives
41 West Locust Street
Bethlehem, Pennsylvania 18018
United States of America
Phone: (610) 866-3255
Fax: (610) 866-9210

The Moravian Archives:
http://www.moravianchurcharchives.org/general.php

Roman Catholic

Archdiocese of Oklahoma City
Pastoral Center Offices
7501 N.W. Expressway
Oklahoma City, OK 73132
Phone: (405) 721-5651
Fax: (405) 721-5210

Archdiocese of Oklahoma City: http://archokc.org/

Diocese of Tulsa
12300E. 91st St., S
Broken Arrow, OK 74012
Phone: (918) 307-4900

Mailing Address
P.O. Box 690240
Tulsa, OK 74169

Diocese of Tulsa: http://www.dioceseoftulsa.org/

Oklahoma Military Records

More than 40 million Americans have participated in some time of war service since America was colonized. The chance of finding your ancestor amongst those records is exceptionally high. Military records can even reveal individuals who never actually served, such as those who registered for the two World Wars but were never called to duty.

Below are a number of links to websites and archives that contain Oklahoma military records.

Oklahoma Historical Society – Oklahoma military casualties from World War I, World War II, Korea and Vietnam, Revolutionary War Pension and Bounty Land-Warrant Applications, Compiled Military Service Records of men who served from the original thirteen colonies, War of 1812 Pension Applications, Civil War Rosters, Civil War Pensions applications.

800 Nazih Zudhi Drive
Oklahoma City, OK 73105
Telephone: 405-522-5225
Fax: 405-521-2492

Oklahoma Historical Society:
http://www.okhistory.org/research/military?full

US Department of Veterans Affairs Nationwide Gravesite Locator – includes information on veterans and their family members buried in veterans and military cemeteries having a government grave marker.

US Department of Veterans Affairs Nationwide Gravesite Locator: http://gravelocator.cem.va.gov/

You may also find your ancestor's military records in the following databases:

United States General Index to Pension Files, 1861-1934:
https://familysearch.org/search/collection/1919699

United States Index to Service Records, War with Spain, 1898:
https://familysearch.org/search/collection/1919583

United States Index to Indian Wars Pension Files, 1892-1926 – military pension records of soldiers who fought in the Indian Wars between 1817 and 1898

United States Index to Indian Wars Pension Files, 1892-1926:
https://familysearch.org/search/collection/1979427

United States Registers of Enlistments in the U.S. Army, 1798-1914 - index of men who enlisted in the United States Army, 1798-1914.

United States Registers of Enlistments in the U.S. Army, 1798-1914: https://familysearch.org/search/collection/1880762

United States Mexican War Pension Index, 1887-1926 - index to Mexican War pension files for service between 1846 and 1848

United States Mexican War Pension Index, 1887-1926:
https://familysearch.org/search/collection/1979390

Civil War Soldiers Service Records - Service records for both Union and Confederate soldiers indexed by soldier's name, rank, and unit.

Civil War Soldier Service Records:
http://go.fold3.com/civilwar_records/

Oklahoma Cemetery Records

As convenient as it is to search cemetery records online, keep in mind that there are a few disadvantages over visiting a cemetery in person. They are:

- Tombstone information is not always accurately transcribed
- The arrangement of the graves in a cemetery can be crucial as family members are often buried next to each other or in the same grave. This arrangement is not always preserved in the alphabetical indexes that are found online.

With that information in mind, the following websites have databases that can be searched online for Oklahoma Cemetery records.

Oklahoma Historical Society – county cemetery records including; cemetery listings, maps, general information and photographs

800 Nazih Zudhi Drive
Oklahoma City, OK 73105
Telephone: 405-522-5225
Fax: 405-521-2492

Oklahoma Historical Society:
http://www.okhistory.org/research/cemetery?full

Tulsa Genealogical Society Library – large collection of cemetery and funeral home records dating from late nineteenth century

9136 East 31st Street
Tulsa, OK 74145
Telephone: 918-627-4224

Tulsa Genealogical Society Library:
http://www.tulsagenealogy.org/library/

Oklahoma Tombstone Transcription Project - death and burial records

Oklahoma Tombstone Transcription Project:
http://www.usgwtombstones.org/oklahoma/oklahoma.html

African American Cemeteries Online – African American, slave, and Native American cemetery records

African American Cemeteries Online:
http://africanamericancemeteries.com/

Access Genealogy – database of Oklahoma cemetery record transcriptions

Access Genealogy:
http://www.accessgenealogy.com/cemetery/oklahoma-cemetery-records.htm

Find a Grave – over 100 million grave records can be searched on this site. Search can be conducted by name, location, or cemetery name.

Find a Grave: http://www.findagrave.com/

Interment.net - A free online database containing approximately 4 million cemetery records from around the world.

Interment.net: http://www.interment.net/

Billion Graves – as the name implies, you can search a billion records including headstone photos, transcriptions, cemetery records, and grave locations.

Billion Graves:
http://billiongraves.com/pages/search/index.php#cemetery

Oklahoma Obituaries

Obituaries can reveal a wealth about our ancestor and other relatives. You can search our **Oklahoma Obituaries Listings** from hundreds of Oklahoma newspapers online for free.

Oklahoma Obituaries Listings:
http://obituarieshelp.org/oklahoma_newspaper_obituaries.html

Oklahoma Wills and Probate Records

The documents found in a probate packet may include a complete inventory of a person's estate, newspaper entries, witness testimony, a copy of a will, list of debtors and creditors, names of executors or trustees, names of heirs. They can not only tell you about the ancestor you're currently researching, but lead to other ancestors.

Probate records in Oklahoma were kept in **Oklahoma County Courts** from the time of each county's creation.

Oklahoma County Courts:
http://www.oscn.net/applications/oscn/start.asp?viewType=COURT
S

You may also find Oklahoma Probate records at:

Oklahoma Historical Society – Oklahoma County probates from 1890-1928

800 Nazih Zudhi Drive
Oklahoma City, OK 73105
Telephone: 405-522-5225
Fax: 405-521-2492

Oklahoma Historical Society:
http://www.okhistory.org/research/genealogy?full

Lawton Public Library – county probates, wills, and deeds dating from 1898

110 S.W. 4th Street
Lawton, OK 73105-3298
Telephone: 405-581-3450

Lawton Public Library:
http://www.cityof.lawton.ok.us/library/genealogy.htm

Family Search has the following online index which can be searched for free:

Oklahoma Probate Records, 1887-2008 link to:
https://familysearch.org/search/collection/2063710

Oklahoma Immigration and Naturalization Records

The naturalization process generated many types of records, including petitions, declarations of intention, and oaths of allegiance. These records can provide family historians with information such as a person's birth date and place of birth, immigration year, marital status, spouse information, occupation, witnesses' names and addresses, and more.

Immigrants to Oklahoma looking to become citizens generally applied at a U.S. District Court, county courthouse, or a district court. You can request copies of declarations, certificates, and other immigration and naturalization records by contacting the clerk's office in individual **Oklahoma County Courts.** For naturalization records after September 1906, contact the **National Archives Southwest Region (Ft. Worth).**

Oklahoma County Courts:
http://www.oscn.net/applications/oscn/start.asp?viewType=COURTS

National Archives Southwest Region (Ft. Worth):
http://www.archives.gov/fort-worth/public/

Oklahoma Native American Records

Tulsa Genealogical Society Library – large collection of Native American records including Indian Marriage records, Native American census records, Indian Pioneer Collection, Native American citizenship records, and much more

9136 East 31st Street
Tulsa, OK 74145
Telephone: 918-627-4224

Tulsa Genealogical Society Library:
http://www.tulsagenealogy.org/library/

Lawton Public Library - Indian-Pioneer History Collection, materials covering the Kiowa, Comanche, and Apache peoples including; census rolls, vital records, and land allotments

110 S.W. 4th Street
Lawton, OK 73105-3298
Telephone: 405-581-3450

Lawton Public Library:
http://www.cityof.lawton.ok.us/Library/gennative.htm

Oklahoma Historical Society – 1896 Applications for Enrolment, Dawes Final Rolls of Five Civilized Tribes

800 Nazih Zudhi Drive
Oklahoma City, OK 73105
Telephone: 405-522-5225
Fax: 405-521-2492

Oklahoma Historical Society:
http://www.okhistory.org/research/genealogy?full

Access Genealogy – Oklahoma Native American census records, tribal histories, and much more

Access Genealogy:
http://www.accessgenealogy.com/native/oklahoma-indian-tribes.htm

U.S. National Archives - information on American Indians who maintained their ties to Federally-recognized Tribes (1830-1970).

U.S. National Archives: http://www.archives.gov/research/native-americans/

Records of the Bureau of Indian Affairs (BIA):
http://www.archives.gov/research/guide-fed-records/groups/075.html

American Indians Records Repository - records dating from the 1700s including trust, education and other historic Indian Affairs records

American Indian Records Repository
Meritex Enterprises
17501 West 98th Street
Lenexa, KS 66219
Phone: 913-888-0601

American Indians Records Repository:
http://www.doi.gov/ost/records_mgmt/american-indian-records-repository.cfm

Missing Matriarchs – Resources for Researching Female Oklahoma Ancestors

Looking for female ancestors requires an adjustment of how we view traditional records sources. A woman's identity was often under that of her husband, and often individual records for them can be difficult to locate. The following resources are effective in locating female ancestors in Oklahoma where traditional records may not reveal them.

<u>Bibliographies</u>

- *Women as Affected by the Laws of Oklahoma,* James Barry King (Oklahoma City n.p.,1930)
- *Women in Oklahoma Territory, 1889-1907,* Janet Hulsly Noever (History Department, Rose State College, 1989)
- *Women of Oklahoma,* Linda Williams Reese (University of Oklahoma Press, 1997)
- *Women in Oklahoma: A Century of Change,* Melvena Thurman (Oklahoma Historical Society, 1982)
- *A Guide to the Indian Tribes of Oklahoma,* Muriel H. Wright (University of Oklahoma Press, 1987)

Selected Resources for Oklahoma Women's History

Museum of the Great Plains
601 Ferris
PO Box 68
Lawton, OK 73502

University of Tulsa
Research in Women's History
600 South College
Tulsa, OK 74104

Pioneer Woman Museum
701 Monument Rd.
Ponca City, OK 74604

University of Oklahoma
Room 452
Monnett Hall
Norman, OK 73109

Common Oklahoma Surnames

The following surnames are among the most common in Oklahoma and are also being currently researched by other genealogists. If you find your surname here, there is a chance that some research has already been performed on your ancestor.

ABERNATHY, ADAMS, ALLEGRE, ALVERSON, ANO, ANOE, BAILEY, BALLENTINE, BEAN, BEAULIEU, BETTS, BICKEL, BLYTHE, BOWEN, BOYER, BROWN, BRYAN, CARTER, CHANEY, CHERRY,CHURCHMAN, COLLIER, COLLYER, COOLEY, COWLEY, COX, CROW, DAVIS, DONNELLY, DOUGLAS, DOUGLASS, DUPREE, DURHAM, ELLIOTT, ENGLEFIELD, ERWIN, FLY, GAINER, GARDNER, GARRESON, GATTIS, GELDER, GOFF, GOODLANDER, GRAY, GRIMES, HALL, HANCOCK, HARRIS, HENDRICKS, HILL, HOLLAND, HOWARD, HOYT, IRVINE, IRWIN, JAQUITH, JOHNSON, JOLLY, JORDAN, KARNER, KEITH, KENNEDY, KENNON, KEY, LANE, LAROCK, LEONARD, LITTLE, LNU, LOCKEY, MACDONNELL, MARTEAU, MATLACK, MATLOCK, MAYS,MCDANIEL, MCDONALD, MCILHANEY, MOORES, MORGAN, MORRIS, NORTON, NORWOOD, O'BRIEN, OSMOND, PARKER, PINEAU, PORTER, POST, RICARD, ROSS, RUSSELL,RUTHERFORD, SCUDDER, SHORT, SIZEMORE, SMART, SMITH, SOOTER, SOOTEUR, SPARKS, SPEAR, STEVENS, STREET, TANKERSLEY, TAYLOR, THOMPSON, TROUT, TURNER, VAN GILDER, , VAN GUILDER, VANGELDER, VANGILDER, VANGUILDER, VINCENT, VINES, WALKER, WARE, WARHURST, WEED, WHITTEN, WILSON, WINCHELL, WUERZ, YOUNG

About the Author

Gary L. Morris worked from 2009 to 2014 as a professional researcher for a major player in the genealogy field. After tracing his family lineage back to 1683, he found that genealogy could be an expensive undertaking. As such, has decided to publish these helpful guides to share the valuable free information he has discovered during his career to help others trace their family lineages as inexpensively as possible. An avid genealogist himself, he hopes you will find this guide factual, thorough, helpful, and most of all, effective in helping you to find your family members.

Notes

Notes

www.ingramcontent.com/pod-product-compliance
Lightning Source LLC
Chambersburg PA
CBHW061930280526
45787CB00004B/1558